GW01606778

The BEARSONIAN INSTITUTION

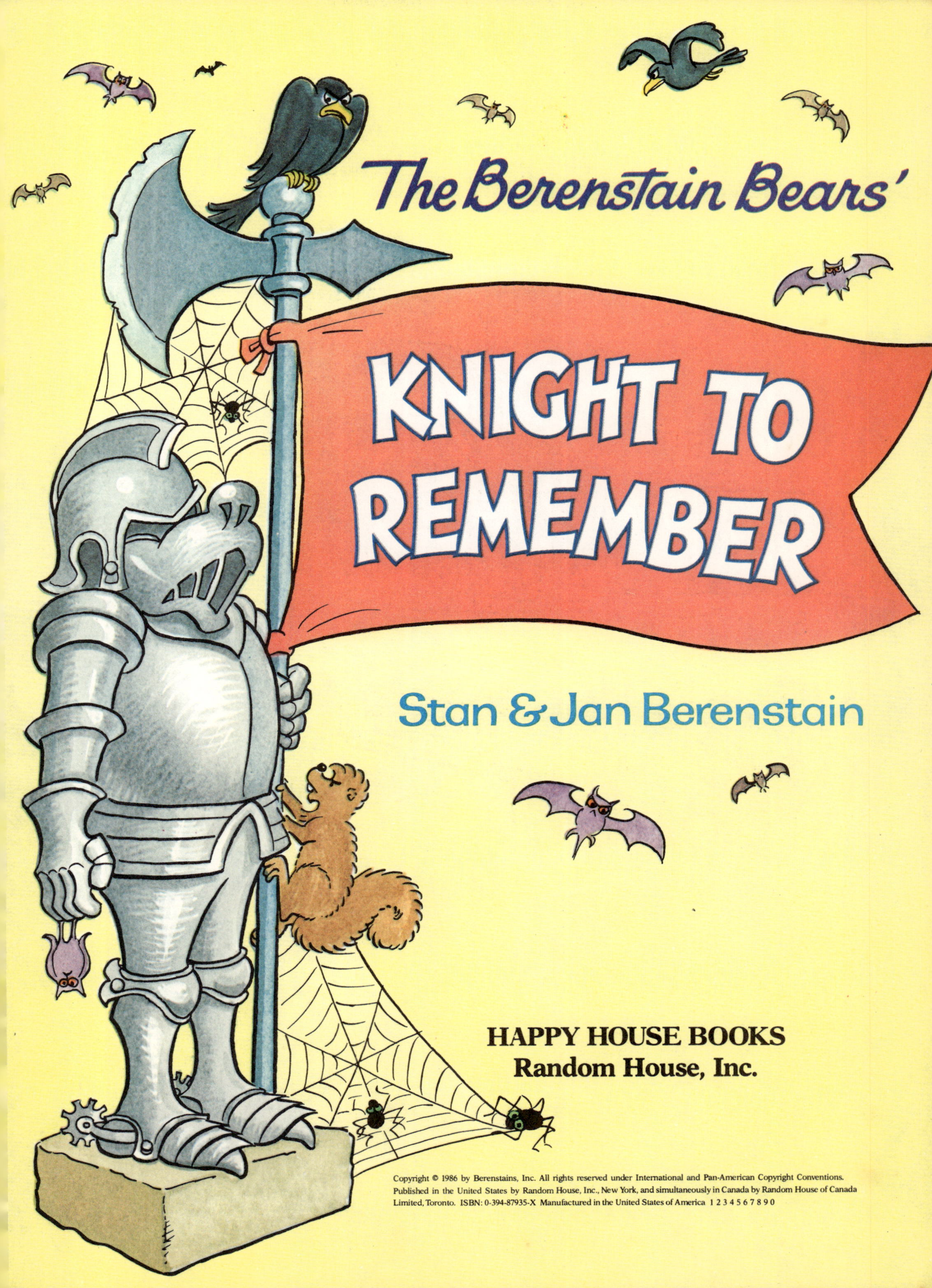
The Berenstain Bears'
KNIGHT TO REMEMBER
Stan & Jan Berenstain
HAPPY HOUSE BOOKS
Random House, Inc.
Copyright © 1986 by Berenstains, Inc. All rights reserved under International and Pan-American Copyright Conventions. Published in the United States by Random House, Inc., New York, and simultaneously in Canada by Random House of Canada Limited, Toronto. ISBN: 0-394-87935-X Manufactured in the United States of America 1 2 3 4 5 6 7 8 9 0

It was a sunny day in Bear Country. Brother Bear was riding his skateboard, and Sister and her butterfly friend were jumping rope when they noticed a new sign on the Shagbark Hickory Bulletin Board.

"'Help Wanted! At Arch-e-o-logical Digs,'" Brother read aloud. "'Apply to Professor Actual Factual.'"

"Archeo-who?" asked Sister.

"It has to do with digging up stuff to find out what happened in olden times," Brother explained.

"Sounds like fun! Let's go help!" Sister said.

"I'll bet tons of bears will be signing up," Brother said.

But the only bear in front of the Bearsonian Institution was Actual Factual. He was sitting sadly on the front steps, and brightened up when he saw the cubs.

"Ah, Brother and Sister Bear! Hardly any visitors come to the museum these days, but I should have known I could count on you," he said.

"That's because the museum's filled with dusty old things," Sister whispered to Brother.

"Maybe we'll find something exciting on the dig," Brother said hopefully.

The professor and the cubs got into the Actual Factual Mobile and drove across the countryside to the archeological site.

Then Actual Factual handed out shovels, picks, and sieves.

"Just remember, there's no such thing as luck in archeology," he said, beginning to dig in the soil. "Sometimes you have to dig for years before you find anything."

Sister lifted up her first shovelful of dirt. "Look—here's something!" she shouted.

“Well, you must have beginner’s luck,” Actual Factual said, examining Sister’s find. “My goodness— you’ve found a real suit of armor, the kind worn by a medieval knight!”

“Complete with battle axe and chains!” Brother said.

“This is indeed a day to remember!” Actual Factual said happily.

“Don’t you mean a *knight* to remember?” Sister asked, giggling.

"Wait—there's something written on the axe blade," Actual Factual said. He looked at it carefully under his magnifying glass.

"Tongue of a toad, eye of a newt,
He who disturbs this armored suit
Shall shiver and shake, and what is worse,
Shall suffer a medieval curse!"

Sister looked scared, while Brother tried to look brave.

"Nonsense!" the professor said. "There's no such thing as a curse. Let's set up this knight in the old tower of the museum. That's the kind of exciting exhibit that ought to bring bears from all over!"

Actual Factual put up a sign announcing the new exhibit in front of the Bearsonian Institution. Then he and the cubs dragged the clanking armor up the steep stairs to the tower room.

"I'll bet nobody's been up here for years," Sister said nervously.

"Nobody except big old spiders and bats!" Brother said.

Actual Factual turned on the light. "Let's put this armor together," he said.

Sister connected the arm pieces to the hand pieces.
Brother connected the shoulders to the body.
And Actual Factual connected the head to the neck.
"Now we *really* have a knight to remember!" he said.

“We’ll hold a grand opening tomorrow,” Actual Factual said. “I’ll serve some of my special crumpets and—”

Suddenly the knight’s axe fell down, slicing one of the crumpets on the table right in half!

“I—I—I thought I saw the gauntlet move,” Brother said.

“And I saw eyes in the visor!” Sister added.

“It was simply an accident,” Actual Factual said firmly. “Time to go home now. I’ll see you here tomorrow, bright and early.”

That night Actual Factual woke to the sound of heavy metal footsteps in the tower room above his apartment in the museum. Then he heard a noise that sounded like clanking chains.

"I'd better go see what's up," he muttered, and climbed out of bed.

When Actual Factual climbed up the tower stairs, what should he see but the knight coming toward him, waving the axe and dragging the chains!

"*Yowwww!*" screamed the frightened professor, and he raced down the steps, ran out of the museum, and streaked off into the night, muttering, "I must cancel the exhibit!"

The next morning Brother and Sister Bear saw the EXHIBIT CANCELED sign in front of the museum.

"It doesn't make any sense," Sister said.

"Yes, it does!" said Actual Factual, popping out from behind the sign. "The curse has come true. The knight is alive! The exhibit's not safe for visitors!"

"I think we should investigate this," Brother said. "Come on!"

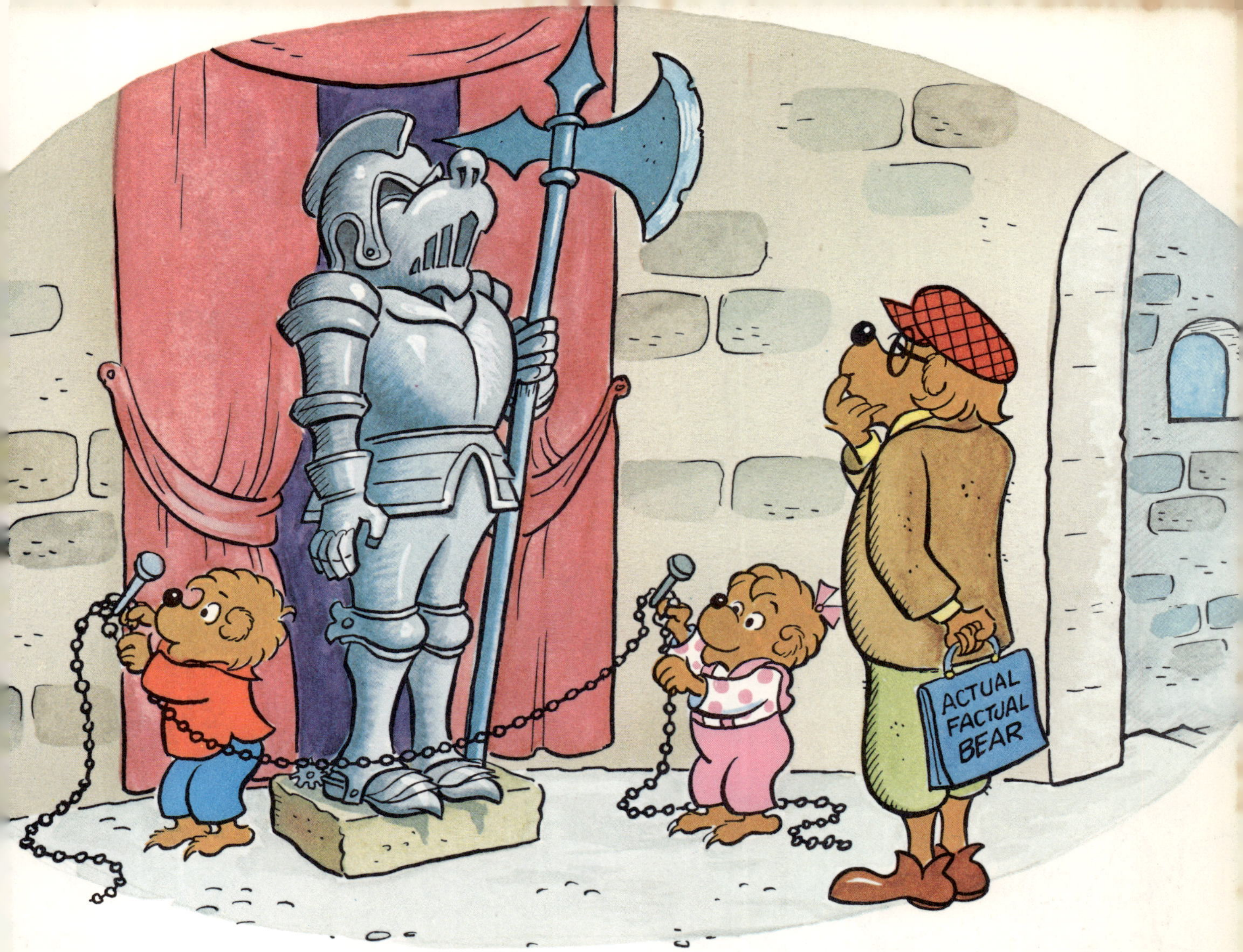

The cubs and the professor tiptoed up the stairs to the tower room. The knight's chain was lying on the floor. Brother and Sister each hooked up an end to a nail on the wall.

"Now for my plan. Start teasing him," Brother whispered. "Hey, over here, you old rust bucket!" he called to the knight.

Sister stuck out her tongue and made faces at the suit of armor.

The knight began to move! It lurched toward the cubs, tripped over the low chain stretched across the room, and crashed to the floor with a loud clatter!

"Look!" cried Brother. "That spider silk is holding the pieces of armor together."

"And those squirrels and crows and bats were pulling the threads so the knight could move," Sister said.

"Well, those animals can't stay here," Actual Factual said. "We must get rid of them."

"But they're just trying to protect their home," Sister said. "I'll talk to them. I'm good at talking with little creatures."

After a few minutes of chatter, Sister turned to Actual Factual. "The insects and animals can stay and make the knight perform for the museum's visitors. It'll be a sensation!"

"Oh my, that sounds wonderful!" Actual Factual said. "I'd better change that 'Canceled' sign right away!"

That day crowds of curious bears streamed into the Bearsonian Institution to view the walking medieval knight.

"That certainly is a knight to remember," one of the bears remarked to Actual Factual.

"That's right, madame," the professor agreed. "But *last* night was pretty exciting too!" And he gave Brother and Sister a big wink.

DON'T MISS
A Knight to Remember
EXCITING NEW EXHIBIT OF MEDIEVAL ARMOR